# Sex in Nature:

## A Guide to Makin
## Me

GU00393993

### Lukasz Luczaj

Illustrations

by Julia Gmosińska

Pietrusza Wola 2020

ISBN 9798639137013

Self-published on Kindle Direct Publishing

Cite this book as: Luczaj, L. 2020. *Sex in Nature: A Guide to Making Love in Forests and Meadows.* Pietrusza Wola: Self-published.

Illustrations by Julia Gmosińska

Cover image: *The temptation of Eve* by Walter Crane, 1899. Credit: Wellcome Collection. Attribution 4.0 International (CC BY 4.0)

Contact with the author:

www.thewildfood.org, www.luczaj.com

# Table of contents

I dedicate my book to

Artemis, the Queen of the Wilderness

My brother Pan

the Moon and Sun

Hyacinth, the lover of Apollo

Narcissus, a boy turned into flower

Promiscuous forest nymphs

And virgins giving themselves to their boys

On wildflower meadows

## Lover

*Behold, you are beautiful, my love.*
*Behold, you are beautiful.*
*Your eyes are doves.*

## Beloved

*Behold, you are beautiful, my beloved, yes, pleasant;*
*and our couch is verdant.*

## Lover

*The beams of our house are cedars.*
*Our rafters are firs.*

— *Song of songs*, 1, 15-17

## Woman

Once I went on a date with a woman. She was just over thirty. Pretty and nice, delicate and petite. She had a good job, she liked yoga and nature. I met her at my workshop about wild edible plants. She took very good pictures, liked colourful autumn leaves and beautiful flowers. Always perfectly dressed. She had a pleasant gentle voice. We started off in a café, but she didn't like it there. I suggested a coffee in an apartment I was renting. She agreed. I didn't really want to make any offers too quickly, but she kept going on about spas and saunas and stuff like that. It sounded kind of steamy.

I just said, "Let's have a bottle of wine. I've bought some Portuguese verde. There's an extra bed, stay overnight."

She replied: "I won't stay, you know how it will end. I don't know you that well. Relax. We can chat for another hour and then I really need to go."

She repeated this five times.

After an hour she did start leaving. But she stopped at the doorway.

"Could you fuck me one day? But not now, in summer."

"I can fuck you now," I replied.

"No, I want to do it when it's warm. I want you to fuck me in your forest. You know, I've never done it in nature. You must know how to do it. You're a botanist! you must know how to fuck in nature."

"Ok, come to my place in summer or even spring. I will fuck you on a meadow full of oxeye daisies and buttercups on a sunny spring day."

"Do you promise?" she said excitedly.

"Promise," I said eagerly.

She never came back. But she gave me the idea to write this book.

## Wildflower meadow

The meadow is a recurring motif in my life. I specialize in making meadow mixes. In 1999 I started collecting wildflower seeds and creating my first flowery grasslands. I lived in the countryside in a run-down wooden cabin with my wife, a small kid, and no money. We wanted to go to the sea for a few days, but we couldn't afford it.

These were the very early days of the internet. I sold seeds by advertising in gardening magazines. People just phoned me, asked questions and placed their orders.

I started collecting seeds in May. In August I put out my first adverts. People started phoning.

It was September and by this time I had a cupboard full of seeds. We were listening to a song by Fisz, a Polish rapper. It was about money falling from the sky like rain. At that very moment, a guy phoned. He had the low, cheerful voice of a dodgy businessman. He ordered a staggering amount. "But that's a lot of money," I warned. "That's not a problem," the guy replied. "You know, I don't mind if it's expensive, but I need beautiful meadows, so beautiful that girls will spread their legs straight away when they see those flowers."

So, we went to the seaside and soon bought a new car with the meadow money.

When I phoned my client a year later to check on the meadow, he said: "Shit, I forgot to sow it!" And he ordered another sack.

## The meadow of love

The notion of erotic play in nature immediately brings southern Europe and Greek and Roman culture to my mind. The love games of Greek gods and goddesses, nymphs and ordinary humans in various formations usually take place in flowery pastures, or close to springs and little brooks.

While writing this book, I found the amazing work of Jo Heirman titled, *The erotic conception of ancient Greek landscapes and the heterotopia of the symposium.* CLCWeb: Comparative Literature and Culture, 2012, 14(3), p.13.

In her paper, Heirman defines what she calls the "meadow of love". It is a frequent setting for erotic scenes in Ancient Greek poetry and mythology. A young virgin being seduced, abducted or raped by a god/satyr/rider is a common motif. Sometimes, the roles are reversed, and a beautiful inexperienced young man is seduced by female goddesses or demons.

These stories inspired painters throughout the ages, from artists of the Renaissance or Pre-Raphaelite era to contemporary times. In more prudent times, Greek mythology was a pretext to show erotic scenes or suggest a sexual act.

One of the most famous stories of this kind is the tale of Hylas and the Nymphs. It was depicted in 1896 by the British painter John William Waterhouse. Now the picture is on display in Manchester Art Gallery. The painting shows the last moments of life of the young Hylas, one of the Argonauts, who set out, led by Jason, from Argo to Colchis in search of the mythical Golden Fleece. Hylas was accompanied by Heracles, who killed Hylas's father, but then took care of the young boy and took him on the quest. When in Mysia, Hylas left the group to bring some water. At a spring, he encountered the Naiads – water nymphs who seduced and then drowned him or kept him a slave. His body was never found. In Waterhouse's painting, the scene is depicted among water lilies, the

Latin name of which is *Nymhaea* – the plant of nymphs!

Although the picture itself does not show a sexual act, the scenes of nudity were shocking enough in themselves at the time it was painted.

The 19th century painting entitled *Le déjeuner sur l'herbe*, sometimes translated as *The Luncheon on Grass*, has been a particularly controversial work of art. It was painted by

Édouard Manet in 1863 and is now on display in the Musée d'Orsay in Paris. The painting shows two nude women and two dressed guys having a picnic on a lawn. It has been met with a lot of criticism over the years, but is a well-known painting in the history of art. For me, it is a manifesto of the contact of our nude bodies with the earth.

Going back to ancient Greece, the mother of European culture... The combination of a flowery meadow and an innocent young person often leads up to abduction. The most famous example is the snatching of Persephone by Hades, as told in the *Hymn to Demeter*. A similar motif is present in a poem by Anacreon (Fragment 417), which I quote in English after Heirman (who in turn quotes Campbell, *Greek Lyric II*, 94-97):

"...why, looking at me from the corner of your eyes, do you flee pitilessly from me and suppose that I have no skill? Let me tell you, I could well put the bit on you, and with the reins in my hand turn you around the race-posts. Instead you graze in meadows and play and leap lightly, since you have no skilful rider, experienced in horses."

Thus, a secluded clearing, a flowery meadow or the bank of a stream can not only be a place of conscious and premeditated pleasure but also a place of danger, as proven by Hylas or Red Riding Hood.

When I hear of Greek mythology and nature, the first creature which comes to my mind is Pan, the God of Nature. He is depicted with hairy legs ending with goat hooves, goat horns and a constantly erect penis. He is the companion of the Nymphs, a symbol of vitality, spring, life and sexuality. His name actually comes from one of the Greek words for pasture! In his person, Pan concentrates many things that civilization has suppressed or forgotten.

I wonder if Pan, with his hairy legs and hooves, attracts or repulses the women who so obsessively remove hair from their legs, armpits and pussies. A wild man is a hairy man! On the other hand, humans have fought against their body hair since prehistoric times. The occupation of a hairdresser is one of the oldest professions of humanity. So Pan, hairy and cruel, is actually not exactly the same as our candy image of depilated lovers smoothly making love on a clean flowery meadow.

# Privacy

Sex is usually an intimate activity. And this is so for most human cultures. Of course, there are exceptions such as ritual orgies. But this is a minority. Usually sex takes place in a quiet and secluded space.

As far as a room is an intimate place for city people in rich countries, in many parts of the world people live in crowded homes. Many people share the same room or shelter. Walls are thin and other members of the family eavesdrop.

Thus, especially for young lovers, nature is an escape – the only place where they can be together relatively freely. I realized this on a train in Sri Lanka, going from Colombo to Candy. When I got my head out of the train, I could see a line of carriages bending along the curves of the hilly route. And along the tracks, between the jungle, hills and the train, there were teenage couples kissing. It was the only place away from their family that they could find.

I assume that a sense of security is important for most people having sex. It is difficult to feel pleasure when afraid of something, when you feel someone might intrude. Women don't reach orgasms and men suddenly lose erections if they hear something unexpected. Of course, the opposite is also possible. Someone can be turned on by such situations, too, but this is slightly rarer. There are two faces to making love in nature: either we might feel secure being far away from people or we may feel kinky, excited by the fact that someone can discover us, like a woman I heard of who could only have an orgasm on a train.

If you really want to be ALONE, avoid paths. Many studies of landscape psychology show that most people stick to paths. No path, no people. Most people never stray more than 10 metres from a path. This rule especially concerns bushy places, where we cannot see very far. People may be quite keen to run through a lawn or a desert. But bushes? No, no, no. They will not risk scratching their dress or calves. Unless they are mushroom pickers, lovers or ornithologists. So, the best place for a love meet-up is be a clump of bushes, but surrounded by open space, so that you are out of sight, but you can see what is happening around you. It's best to be on a small hill. That way you will feel like you're in a small stronghold.

**Will I go to prison for this?** This a very serious question. **In many places of the world, if you are discovered having sex in a place that someone treats as public or theirs, you may not only go to prison but even die.** So, I advise you make sure you know the law. A safe place might be a private fenced forest or a big garden in a liberal country. Any deviations from that may cause trouble, starting with a court fine. Also think of other people, try not to upset anyone or hurt their sense of decency. This book is not for flashers! And don't get caught!

Recently Polish media reported a case of a couple who was fined for having sex in a private forest. The owner installed a hidden camera to catch people dumping trash from cars into his forest. Instead, he captured people having sex. The Polish law punished the offenders, following §140 of the Polish Code of Offences, with a fine of up to 1500 PLN (the equivalent of 400 US Dollars), nearly the monthly minimum salary in my country. Bear in mind that the owner of this forest only reported the case to the police because they kept leaving tissues and condoms!

# Forest

*The writer Lubinski stated that the ageless forest makes men helpless dreamers who disappoint women. The forest overpowers you with its abysmal depth, swings you and makes you fall asleep with the rustling of branches, it terrifies you with its ageless existence.*

> — Zbigniew Nienacki, *Raz do roku w Skiroławkach [Once a year in Skiroławki]*, my translation from Polish

The forest is the first choice for lovers in many parts of the globe. However, having made love in different kinds of forest – in deciduous woods, in coniferous taiga, in bamboo thickets or a primeval rainforest – I can see that what KIND of forest it is makes a difference.

In Poland or Russia, for example, pine is the most common species of tree. However, pine is not that good for lovers, apart from the fresh smell of their needles and branches caused by essential oils. You should generally avoid pines.

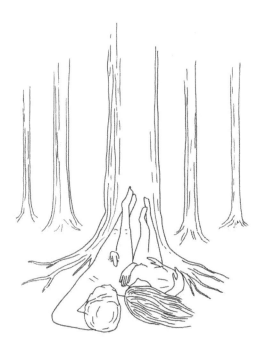

Why? First of all, pinewoods are full of cones. They are hard and will get into your back and bum. Pine bark is rough and will scratch your back if you rest on it.

Pinewoods are full of resin, which will glue to your feet. They give very little shade. In summer, you will be boiling under pine canopy. However, this may be an advantage in September on a cooler day when you will be happy to catch some sun rays.

Due to lack of shade, pinewoods on fertile soil are full of understory thickets, brambles and the like. Again, this is not too pleasing to lovers.

I much prefer spruce forests. They give a lot of shade and smell just as nice. Their needles are softer, and their bark is softer too. So, there are only needles or moss on the floor of old spruce woods. The only minus is that dark shady spruce forests are quite sad and often riddled with mosquitoes.

What about deciduous trees? Well, it all depends on the part of the world. But if do you happen to be in the temperate zone on a warm day, you will have bedding made of the soft and small leaves of beech, oak, hornbeam or maple at your disposal. Wait… Oak is not always that soft. But it will do.

I adore trees with slippery bark, such as beeches (*Fagus*) and hornbeams (*Carpinus*) in temperate forests and many fig (*Ficus*) species in the jungle. They are pleasant to touch, rub, press against, hug. A fallen beech tree is a treasure for lovers. They are so smooth that a naked person can sit on them. If a woman's labia are large and stick out, the beech will not harm them. After the rain you can even slide on the beech. Unfortunately, this is a valuable tree and large fallen specimens are quickly removed by foresters, unless it grows on a wild mountainside or in an English park.

When writing about beeches, I must mention their use as love magic in Silesia near Cieszyn (Polish-Czech border). For this purpose, you need to look for a beech tree that grows so close to a fir tree that when the wind blows, the two trees scratch against each other.

Tear off some bark from this place, burn it and add it to a person's drink. This will cause them to fall madly in love with you. I found this charm in "Słownik Fischera" [*Fischer's Dictionary*], a pre-World War II manuscript, which I coedited with Monika Kujawska and two other colleagues (Kujawska M, Łuczaj Ł, Sosnowska J, Klepacki P. *Rośliny w wierzeniach i zwyczajach ludowych: słownik Adama Fischera.*

Wrocław: Polskie Towarzystwo Ludoznawcze; 2016).

Oak forests have a different energy. Their trunks are rougher, and the leaves harder. They also give less shade, so they are something between beech and pine forests. The leaves, although hard, are nice in touch. And the leaves and branches smell of tannins. Making love on the floor of an oak forest is like making love in a tea box or whiskey barrel.

Lime trees (also called lindens) rarely become a dominant tree in woods, more often they occur as an admixture. However, they are often planted in gardens, parks and along roadsides. They used to be important shade trees in many regions of Europe due to the pleasant smell they produce (even the wood is fragrant), especially during flowering time. The herbal tree from linden flowers was so important that the month of July in Polish and the month of June in Croatian are named after it, and the Croatian currency, *lipa*, is also named after the tree. The famous song "Under

der linden" is a poem written in Middle High German by the medieval lyric poet Walther von der Vogelweide. It starts with the following lines:

*Under the lime tree*
*On the heather,*
*Where we had shared a place of rest,*
*Still you may find there,*
*Lovely together,*
*Flowers crushed and grass down-pressed.*
*Beside the forest in the vale…*
        (translated by Raymon Oliver)

In the third stanza the song says that the lover " …had fashioned /For luxury / A bed from every kind of flower."

Are there any types of forest which are useless for lovers? There certainly can be: spiny thickets or a forest overrun by nettles, for example. Also avoid the company of blackthorn. A lot of people report that blackthorn wounds are hard to heal. However, one person told me they lost their virginity under a big blackthorn bush in an overgrown English hedge.

Please avoid black locust (*Robinia pseudoacacia*) forests. This tree from the American Appalachians is now very common in central Europe, for example in parts of Slovakia, Hungary or Romania. The tree is spiny, and you can get hurt by its thorns lying on the ground. Unfortunately, the more you go to dry and hot climates, the more thorns you will encounter. It is just that plants use thorns to protect themselves more in places where growth is made difficult by drought. Going to the dry subtropical zone, you will find spiny cacti, spiny tree stems and spiny vines. Better be careful and sit on a banana leaf if you can find one.

But going back to deciduous woods in general… They are best in spring, before the leaves develop. Like photographers have their golden hour, when the afternoon sun gives gold softness to images, forests have their golden time for lovers just before leaves develop. These are the long days when it gets suddenly warm, when trees are blossoming, when various bluebells, anemones, snowdrops, or primroses are out – depending on the specific geographic area and timing. In my Carpathian forests in southern Poland, this golden time usually happens at the end of April. In this season, the ground in some of the beechwoods is completely covered with flowers. Sometimes this time also coincides with the mass flowering of wild cherries (*Prunus avium*) in the forests.

There are quite a few species you might mean by cherries (*Prunus avium, P. fruticosa, P. cerasus,* etc.). The Japanese have their Sakura – the holiday of oriental cherries (*P. serrulata*) and blossom in general. The Japanese make picnics under cherry trees, sit and drink under them. For us lovers of sex in nature, the time of blossoming is a kind of Sakura too. We associate blossom with gardens, but in some parts of the world woods are covered with wild apple, pear, cherry, almond or quince blossom, depending on the area of the world. Springtime sex is wonderful – no mushroom pickers, no mosquitoes, flies or other insects. Only in the Mediterranean you might encounter asparagus pickers or people foraging for other wild vegetables. So, beware and don't forget to take a basket of wine, camembert and a baguette with you. Sit under a blooming cherry tree and bless your life!

It sometimes happens that "the Golden Days" come much earlier. Once I made love in February, on a warm 15 °C day. We sat under a sycamore tree. The sap of sycamores, maples and birches had already started flowing up the trunks. One cut with a knife, a branch would shoot with fresh, sweetish sap. The pre-springtime, when sap starts buzzing inside trees, is very magical for me. You can feel a tension, waiting, concentration of nature. Soon, in a week or a month, it will fully shoot with life. This time is wonderfully depicted by Julian Tuwim's poem *Brzozy* (*Birches*) starting from the following stanza:

*I will open the birches' veins with my axe.*
*I will cut through their body, scratch their roots.*
*I will soil them with their own sticky sap.*
*I will jump with my mouth to their white wounds.*

(my translation from Polish)

Of course, there are thousands of tree species and hundreds of types of forests. Some trees, like the eucalyptus, have an amazing smell. However, this genus has quite stiff and sharp leaves. It really depends on the part of the world you are in. In some areas, most plants will be hard or spiny.

Mediterranean vegetation is difficult for lovers. It is often composed of maquis, a tangle of spiny shrubs, climbers, thorny asparagus and the like. There's no way you can get through it. At least it smells beautiful. You could maybe find some forgotten stony path. Look for pastures: they are often overgrown by thistles, but there's always some nice soft spot with wild thyme to be found. And the Mediterranean climate makes up for this. You may also find some shade under an old olive tree with cyclamens flowering around you. Making love under an olive tree is like making love under a willow. There's a similar feeling to it; a similar soft energy is conjured up by its elliptical leaves. The richness of etheric oils in Mediterranean herbs can really make you feel like a lover from the Biblical Song of Songs:

*A locked-up garden is my sister, my bride;*
*a locked-up spring,*
*a sealed fountain.*
*Your shoots are an orchard of pomegranates, with precious fruits:*
*henna with spikenard plants,*
*spikenard and saffron,*
*calamus and cinnamon, with every kind of incense tree;*
*myrrh and aloes, with all the best spices*

— *Song of Songs*, 4, 12-14

## Leaves

We had not seen each other for a few months. We met in a café. We had decided to stop seeing each other. We were only going for a coffee this time, but I could see how her animal nature was calling me. I could see how she thrust out her chest forward and curled cusps of hair around her finger. Her hair was long as a horse mane.

"Shall we go for a walk?" I proposed.

"Yes, that's a very good idea, I was just about to propose it."

It took half an hour to get out of the city. I didn't know the area too well. I hoped we would not end up in a pinewood with thick undergrowth, full of nettles and brambles. But we found an old growth beechwood, smooth and soft like a carpet.

The forest was on a slope, so when lying down, we felt as if we were sitting in armchairs. We were both dressed very formally. I took my suit and white shirt off and she took off her dark jacket and white shirt, too. We both had some important stuff to sort out, we didn't usually dress like that. It was as if we specially wore these clothes for this forest. We hung up our white shirts on a large elder bush, as if to symbolize surrender. It was a warm October day, and we fell into the autumn leaves. We were all covered by beech, oak and hornbeam leaves. They stuck to our hair and skin. I threw them up in the air one by one. She looked like a lady from a Pre-Raphaelite painting. It's a shame she was not red-haired. A large oak leaf got right into her vulva. Luckily, it was not an acorn, or I would have been jealous.

# Trees

Trees are one of the staples for eroticism in the forest. They let you free yourself from often humid and cold ground, from the earth full crawling dangers. The first time I had sex with the help of a tree, it was in the standing position. It was March, with patches of snow still covering in the ground, and first woodland flowers, like wood anemones (*Anemone nemorosa*) and corydalis (*Corydalis solida*), were emerging from between the leaves. We stopped the car in the night in a place where the land was cutting through a forest. The trees were mainly beech, very smooth. We made love standing. Having sex propped by a tree is OK if you're of matching height. But quite often you won't be, and the shorter person will have to stand on something. In nature you will have to find a large stone or a log, so it's a hassle. A good solution is something called the lumberjack position, with the woman propping against the tree and the man entering her from behind.

Large toppled tree logs are a real treasure. There are so many options here. You can sit on the log, you can lie on it, you can treat it like a chair or like a bench.

The quality of bark is essential – rough bark may be uncomfortable. It will scratch your back and may even cut your genitals. In temperate climates, beech and hornbeam are perfect, whereas oak and pine are usually rough. Some species are rough at the base and smooth at the top. This is the case with birches and aspens. However, the latter have much longer smooth stretches from the former. They also grow faster, so they have sizeable trunks. If you can't distinguish between species of trees, just be aware of these differences and go for the smooth ones.

Logs are rarely left lying in private or state forests used for harvesting wood. But sometimes you can spot one, usually far from roads. National parks on the other hand abound in them. The most natural forest of the European lowland – the Białowieża Forest on the edge of Poland and Belarus – is amazing for erotic play. There are gigantic fallen trunks everywhere. Technically you are not allowed to enter the main part of the park without a licensed guide, but there are other areas with a less strict protection regime, far enough from any paths and never frequented by humans.

There are also trees at weird angles, sometimes 45 degrees. They are as comfy as armchairs, very good for the ordinary missionary frontal position.

## Hollow tree

Finding a hollow tree is like finding an abandoned tent. No one can see you, everyone can hear you. Hollow trees for couples do exist, but they are rare, much rarer than fallen trees. There's one such tree in the centre of the city of Rzeszów. It is a 200-year-old plane tree in a park by the castle. Another is an old oak in a park in Zimna Woda near Jasło. If you are based around London there is a hollow beech in the centre of Hampstead Heath.

Entrances are usually narrow. You have to stand, or one person stands and another crouches. And obviously neither of you should be scared of spiders. There are always both spiders and spider webs around. Some of these creatures can bite. In temperate climates, it might feel like a bee sting, but in Australia I would be careful… And once a bat flew right into my face.

## Learning to walk

We met in a cafe in a small town north from Rzeszów in rural Poland. It was a beautiful sunny day, early May. The whole of nature had just woken up. She was a cute girl with a beautiful face and delicate, dainty body. Our conversation wasn't really flowing.

"Let's go for a walk," she said.

She wanted to show me some forest path which had recently been covered with asphalt. This made it the perfect place for her to roller-skate.

"Why don't we go into the Forest?" I asked. "Look, I'm wearing new shoes, they'll get damaged."

"Take them off!"

"I don't know, I've never thought of walking barefoot in the forest."

And she took them off. She was scared to walk through the woods on her own. I had to hold her hand like someone who helps a person who is recovering after breaking a leg, or like a parent teaching their child to walk.

It was the first time in her 26-year old life that the soles of her feet had touched cones and needles. She walked slowly, like someone walking on a rope. Like a dancer holding her skirt.

She walked maybe a dozen steps, sat down and cried. "Why haven't I done this before? Why did I spend all those years in shoes?" she said.

## Mosses and edges

Moss is a blessing for lovers. How did nature come to create something so pleasant to lie and sit on? It is a ready-made bed. Nothing more to add, apart from the fact that you can usually find it in dark and damp woods, which are not ideal for taking your clothes off. And the moss absorbs a lot of moisture.

Forest edges are better places. Here the leaf litter layer is always smaller, as the wind tends to blow the leaves away. This supports rich moss life even in dryer woods. The Polish botanist Romuald Olaczek called this abundance of mosses on forest edges "bryophitization" (bryophyte is the scientific name for mosses and liverworts).

Forest edges are magical places for a variety of reasons. They are sunnier, and the branches and trunks of trees grow at a variety of angles, which gives you more choices for "on the tree" positions.

Talking about trees and branches... Yet another interesting item can be a log lying across a small valley or ravine, hanging one or two meters in the air. They are often overgrown by mosses and look like a green bridge for elves or dwarves. If broad enough and climbable, they create another interesting platform for sex.

I remember one walk on the island of Saaremaa in Estonia. It was dry then, during the midsummer period when days are very long, lasting nearly 24 hours. Even the sphagnum moss in the spruce forests were dry. We could lie on the soft cushions of *Sphagnum, Leucobryum* and *Polytrichum* mosses. It was quite dark under the spruces, but rays of sun penetrated the forest floor here and there. And we lay in this scenery. We lay and talked about plants, herbs and aquarium fish. Just resting quietly for two hours. This peaceful romantic conversation was going to transform into a two-year stormy relationship that would shake my entire life later on. After the forest walk, we went to an Estonian sauna.

The north of our globe is full of peat bogs. You can find them for example in Canada, Scotland, Scandinavia and Russia. A peat bog is a wet area overgrown by sphagnum moss in a pine forest clearing you might find in Siberia, Canada or Northern Europe. Walking on it is like walking on a sponge. The water is still, and it does get warm on a quiet sunny summer day. Actually, two people to whom I told about writing this book mentioned the "magic of a peat bog" in their erotic memories. It is a special place indeed. You lie on the peat, slightly submerged in brown whiskey-coloured and whiskey-smelling water. It's like lying on a mattress from IKEA... If you can orgasm before the 1000th mosquito arrives – you will enjoy it.

However, sex in water is generally over-rated. I do love sex in the forest and meadows, but water I think is third grade for me. We are clearly animals of the savannah.

My favourite position in water is standing knee-deep or half-hip deep. Or find a tree stump on the edge of the river. Or lean out of your canoe. Anyway, I must warn you that many people won't make love in water out of fear of leeches or being nibbled by fish.

## Midsummer night

As a young boy, I once visited a particularly beautiful meadow. It was a flat grassland, adjacent to a large stream called Jasiołka, in the Beski Niski hills, between Tylawa and Daliowa. On the other side of the river, there was a nearly vertical mountain slope covered by primeval forest. The meadow was cut once a year, a perfect balance of vertical and horizontal, closed and open. It was a place like those cigarette adverts shot in Yellowstone or Utah. The best of the best.

Later this place always haunted me in my erotic dreams. One day, many years later, it so happened that they became reality. It was a midsummer night. She was wearing a stripy t-shirt. We held hands and started walking through a small path surrounded by a large area of young birch and alder undergrowth, which separated it from the road. We carefully avoided brambles. The meadow was in the peak of flowering. If you are a phyto-sociologist, you will understand more when I say that it was something between an *Arrhenatherion*, *Nardion* and a *Molinion* meadow. Flowers spread to the horizon. Oxeye daisies, yellow rattle, betony, hair bell, ragged robin, field scabious, knapweed and even St. John's wort, wild thyme and the like. This was a mountain meadow, not so fertile, so everything was pleasantly low. There was only one tree, a birch, in the very middle. We lay down. I could smell her sweat, mixed with fragrance of thyme, a gentle after-smell of coumarin from grass and a bitter trace of St. John's wort. I was looking over her thighs at the red sunset when I spotted a small figure of an animal. It was a wolf. We were staring at each other in near silence, the grasshoppers had already started their concert.

When you saw the title of the chapter, the Midsummer, you probably imagined I was going to start writing about midsummer orgies. But no – I wanted you to look at the simplest of things, the beauty of the union of our body, nature and this magic moment, regardless if it is mid-summer or a school holiday. The power of the moment could have been similar for a lonely masturbating traveller.

In the Slavic tradition, midsummer was a special time when ordinary social taboos stopped existing. When you could do more. How much more, we do not know. Nowadays people in Poland imagine that in pre-Christian pagan times people organized orgies there, but who knows, maybe it was just a sheer loosening of everyday behaviour... What we imagine was an orgy may have been more freedom in people talking, touching, or kissing. Anyway, this time is associated with special erotic energy, which is expressed in beliefs about plants.

In Slavic dialects, some plants were called "brother and sister" as people believed they were siblings turned into flowers for incestual sex during midsummer. In some parts of Europe these were pansies, in others wood cow-wheat (*Melampyrum nemorosum*). This issue is discussed in detail by Kazimierz Moszyński in his *Kultura ludowa Słowian* [*Folk culture of Slavs*]. Both species have mixed yellow-purple flowers. The yellow is the brother, the purple is the sister. This belief was very widespread – it was held all the way from Poland, across the Baltic Nations, Belarus to Russia.

Even today, a midsummer night, or any warm summer night with a bonfire party, may be the only time when people have sexual experiences outdoors, far from the house, garden or pavement, etc.

Another plant we should seek on a midsummer night is adder's tongue *Ophioglossum vulgatum.* It is a fern that does not look like a fern. It lacks the characteristic divided fine leaves. The leaf is simple and is accompanied by a stalk with spores. Altogether it looks like a green calla-type flower or a plantain. It is amazing that people in the Polish countryside, hundreds of years ago, figured out that it is a kind of fern. Central

Europe is rife with stories of a flowering fern blooming only on Midsummer night or at Christmas. And in Poland, the flowering fern usually meant adder's tongue. A lot of magic powers were attributed to this plant. The plant is very small and easy to overlook in grass swards. It was believed that adder's tongue opened all locks. It also brought immense luck in love. The following love charm was uttered while collecting the plant:

*Nasięźrzale, nasięźrzale,*
*Rwę cię śmiale,*
*Pięcią palcy, szóstą, dłonią,*
*Niech się chłopcy za mną gonią;*
*Po stodole, po oborze,*
*Dopomagaj, Panie Boże.*

*Adder's tongue, adder's tongue,*
*I bravely collect you,*
*With five fingers, with the sixth hand;*
*Let boys chase me,*
*Around the barn, around the shed,*
*Let God help.*

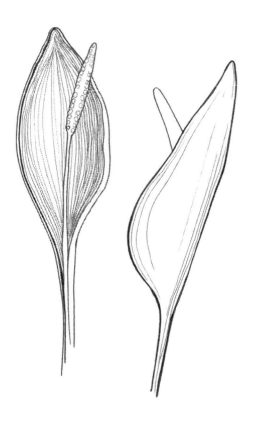

And what happened if a girl, after midsummer night, wanted to be a virgin again? The 17th century herbal of Sirennius is full of information about piquant uses of herbs. One of these is lady's mantle. Its Polish name is *przywrotnik,* which can be translated as "bringer-back", as its astringent properties helped to bring back lost virginity. It worked by causing parts of a woman's vulva to shrink and tighten. It was used for compresses and women took baths in its infusion. As a result, "you could not tell those who lost virginity from real virgins" (Sirennius, vol. 1, p. 328).

## Folk love

In the beginning of the book, when I mentioned ancient Greece, I wrote about the dangers of being alone in a woodland clearing. The same motif appears in Polish folklore. The richness of the Polish country love story can be seen in the ethnographic monograph *Miłość ludowa* [*Folk Love*], written by Dobrosława Wężowicz-Ziółkowska (Wężowicz-Ziółkowska D. Miłość ludowa: wzory miłości wieśniaczej w polskiej pieśni ludowej XVIII-XX wieku. Polskie Towarzystwo Ludoznawcze; 1991). The author studies in detail a situation in which there is usually a young girl who lives in a territory uninhabited by other humans. She lists the most common situations in which she meets the lover:

- She is a shcpherdess and manages cattle, geese, ducks or pigs by a lake, in a forest, behind a wood, over a hill.

- She collects something like berries or fodder in a forest or on the land that belongs to a lord.

- She fetches water from a spring or a well.

She further gives examples of love songs that describe these stories, but the rhymes do not translate well into English, so I will skip them. In another part of her monograph (p. 178), Wężowicz-Ziółkowska also defines the typical meeting places of secret lovers in the countryside. These are:

- in the forest

- in thickets, scrubs, coppices, riverside willow bushes and the like

- in a woodland clearing

- at the edge of the cultivated land

- over a hill

- in a meadow, in a haystack

- in an orchard or garden.

# Wild thyme

Wild thyme reminds me of pubic hair. It forms cushions shaped exactly like the mons pubis. This English medical term comes directly from Latin and means the mountain of the lap/genital area. In north European meadows wild thyme often grows on anthills, making this an even more apt comparison.

In Polish and most other Slavic languages, the names for wild thyme, e.g. *macierzanka, macierduszka*, derive from the word mother. Why? Because it was an important herb for healing infections of female urinary and genital tracts. It was also used in a similar way for animals, e.g. cows. So, wild thyme is the herb of mothers, women and female creatures of all mammal species in general. In some European countries, girls would make wreaths made from wild thyme and put them under their pillows at night to dream of the future husband.

Wild thyme does not grow in hay meadows. You can only find it in dry places, often pastures. Why? Because it is a short, slowly growing plant. In fertile meadows, it is easily overgrown by taller plants, especially grasses. But when animals graze, they leave out the aromatic herbs like thyme, oregano, savory or sage. That is why pastures are the bucolic paradise of lovers. Animals are caretakers of this lawn. They graze vegetation low so that it is nice to walk on the grass and easy to lay on it. The pasture is a sunny and pleasant place. Trees are often left in pastures so that animals have shade, while in ordinary hay meadows they are an obstacle for cutting the grass, especially in the age of tractors. Lovers can use the shade of the trees of pastureland just like the sheep do. But pastures can vary. Some might be neglected and overgrown with thorny bushes, brambles, nettles and thistles.

A place of pleasure for the lover is a place of work for the shepherd. People who took care of their herds in the mountains often had to abandon their families for several months, leaving their wives and children in the valleys. Sexual abstinence during this time could lead to unusual behaviour. Not without reason, some sheep herding countries were given the vulgar epithet of 'sheep-shaggers'. Such things did happen among some shepherds. Nowadays sex with animals is criminalized, but once it was probably seen more as an alternative to masturbation or same sex acts for shepherds. And it does appear in literature, for example in "The Painted Bird" by Jerzy Kosiński (1965), a semi-fictitious story of the escape of a Jewish boy during World War II. At some point of his Odyssey, he stays in a farmer family in the marshes. One night he sees a girl having sex with a goat. A woman from Michel Houellebecq's *Serotonin* loves having sex with dogs of various pedigrees. I have also heard a few stories from doctors and nurses about cases of girls having sex with large dogs, like German shepherds, getting clenched and having to be taken to hospital.

Bodil Joensen (1944-1985) is sometimes described as an exemplary zoophile and became famous for her long-lasting relationships with her pigs. This Danish actress was an animal lover. She ran a small farm and has some sort of celebrity status due to her numerous pornographic films in which she engaged in sex with animals. Unfortunately, she died from neglect, in despair after her pigs were euthanized.

We humans are lucky to be one species. But in some taxonomic groups, the transition between species is a continuum, and individuals have to make choices… Once in an anthropology lecture I told students about the biological differences and similarities between *Homo sapiens* and bonobo chimpanzees (*Pan paniscus*), whose Latin name was inspired by god Pan I mention in the beginning of this book. Out of curiosity, I asked the students if they would agree to take part in an experiment of having intercourse with a chimpanzee in order to create a human-ape hybrid if someone gave them a million dollars. I did not inform them about the differences in chromosome numbers which make it highly unlikely. I said it as a joke, a kind of rhetorical question, without expecting any response. But quite a few female students said they would do it, as they didn't see much difference between their male colleagues and apes anyway.

Are women more open to interspecies sex? I do not think so, taking into the account the aforementioned shepherds, as well as accounts from Amazonia about a river dolphin, ini (*Inia geoffrensis*), known in Jívaro languages as apuupu. Jívaro Quechua and Mestizo share a belief that inis' vaginas are similar to human ones (Brown MF 1986. *Tsewa's Gift: Magic and Meaning in an Amazonian Society*. Smithsonian Institution Press, Washington & London). Brown was told a story about a man who had sex with an ini and it was so pleasant that he developed a habit for it.

## Adorning the body

Forest flowers and fruits can become an additional adornment for lovers. Strawberry and rowan fruits can be stuck on a string or a grass stalk to make "wild necklaces". According to Adam Fischer's dictionary, there were many superstitions associated with rowan in the eastern borderlands of Poland. For example, around Lwów, girls used rowan roots to incite love.

Petals stuck to eyelids to look like flowery eye lashes are another natural adornment. Some flowers easily glue to them, but you have to try many species, as few will have these properties. In the Polish flora a species of bell, *Campanula patula,* and meadow cranesbill, *Geranium pratense,* will work. Fingers can be adorned by foxglove flowers (*Digitalis purpurea*). The name of this plant suggests the flowers are worn by foxes, but the true etymology is they were the folks' gloves ('fairy folks').

Flower wreaths or wreaths made from fragrant leafy branches, such as bay leaves that were used in ancient Greece, are another ad-hoc body decoration.

## Wheat and bushes

Quite a few Polish movies show lovers hidden in cereal fields: wheat, rye or oats. *Nad Niemnem* (1987) directed by Zbigniew Kuźmiński and *Sami swoi* (1967) by Sylwester Chęciński are good examples. In a monotonous lowland landscape of Poland, in which arable fields dominated the view, trees were often only somewhere on the horizon. The actual etymology of Poland is "the land of fields" (*pole* is Polish for field). Pastures and meadows were closely cut. In July, when it was hot and lovers could make love outside, hay meadows had already been cut and you could not hide in them, so only cereals were tall enough to give some privacy. Until recently, cereals such as wheat were taller, reaching up to people's waist, as people were a few inches shorter. Now new crop varieties have shorter stalks and the height of cereals is half of what it used to be. In the past, if you crawled in wheat or rye, it felt like a tunnel. As a kid I used to trample my neighbour's cereals and hide in them. The fields were not sprayed with chemicals, so crops were mingled with colourful weeds such as red poppies, blue cornflowers, violet corn cockles and various kinds of chamomile, and you would get tangled in the colourful twining stalks of vetch. What love must have been like between rye, chamomile, and poppy! I was born too late! By the time I became an adult, the weeds had disappeared, and the cereal stalks had shortened.

The old inhabitants of Warsaw would say that "sex in the wilderness" for them meant hiding in willow bushes along the river Wisła (Vistula), which is the largest Polish river that runs through the capital, and never used to be as overgrown as it is now. In the past, there were more bushes than trees growing on its banks. The same goes for other rivers that ran through agricultural areas. Osiers (a kind of willow) were used to stabilize the banks, for making baskets and bean supports. By hiding inside these bushes, you can become kind of invisible, even in cities and city parks. In Warsaw, walking alongside the osiers also equalled to the likelihood of encounters with drunks and prostitutes.

Now the valley is deeply overgrown by tall trees, willows, poplars and invasive box elders (*Acer negundo*). The trees and bushes are covered by hops and other climbers, such as hedge bindweed (*Calystegia sepium*) and American wild cucumber (*Echinocystis lobata*). Even the clearings are covered by very tall herbs that reach up to the neck, such as the invasive Canadian goldenrod (*Solidago canadensis*) and Himalayan balsam (*Impatiens glandulifera*). The golden rod's plumed fruits are a nuisance – they attach themselves to your trousers, jumper, coat or body hair, making wading through this thicket really annoying.

But Warsaw's wild flood plain forest has its magic. You can still hide in the centre of a city with a population of two million. You could have sex inside this forest, sitting on the low, nearly vertical branches of an old box elder. Or you can make it all the way to the river. In some places, the bank is covered by larger boulders. In other places, when the water is low enough, it uncovers sandy beaches. There are anglers here and there, but lovers can still succeed and find a spot unattended by humans for a few hours.

A friend of mine developed a habit of making love with her boyfriend under the cover of large bushy yew trees in the royal park of Łazienki, in the centre of Warsaw, just opposite the Prime Minister's Palace.

The degree to which you want to engage in having sex in urban nature islands depends on what you want from the wilderness. Do you want peace and beauty, or the excitement of doing something furtive and not completely legal?

## Making a bed

We can make love on the ground, in mud, on a tree. But maybe we could just make a bed in the wilderness, instead of carrying a blanket?

In the past, duvets were often filled with hay or other dry plants. In Poland, such a hay duvet was called *siennik*. Oak leaves and bracken were collected as bedding for animals in barns. How do you make a bed in the forest? Well, it all depends in which part of the world you are…

In Central Europe, fir (*Abes alba*) is a good choice. It has flat soft needles and its smaller branches make for a really soft bedding. It smells of Christmas. When I started living in the countryside in 1997, we slept on such a pile of branches for two years! I changed them every 2-3 months when they were getting dry. We stabilized the edges of this bed with large poles. Similar beds of conifer branches were made by some Native American warriors (e.g.

Crow tribe) on hilltops when they fasted for a few days for their Vision Quest.

To go back to our fir bed in the house: the expression on the faces of our guests when they entered the house was priceless. One day, on a warm June night, I collected a few hundred fireflies and threw them round the room. When we switched off the light, the room was lit up with them.

The yew tree also has soft branches, but it is deadly poisonous. I believe it is not the best for bedding and it was believed that even sleeping under a yew tree could cause death.

In England, in the old days, lady's bedstraw (*Galium verum*) is said to have been used to make bedding, as the name implies. The plant has a nice coumarin scent of hay but is too hard to use without an insulating cloth. In Scotland beds were made from heather (*Calluna vulgaris*). Bracken (*Pteridium aquilinum*) and other ferns are very soft and good for bedding. However, you have to be careful with bracken as it is highly carcinogenic. Tree leaves are great, for example those of oak, maple or beech.

A few armfuls of dry grass will do. Just be careful not to collect the sharp ones, which easily make cuts on your skin.

# Stinkhorn

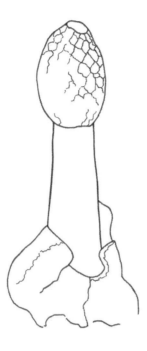

Common stinkhorn's scientific name is *Phallus impudicus,* Latin for impudent phallus – an impudent dick. And not without reason. It looks like a large erect dick sticking out on the forest floor. What's more, it has a strong odour, designed to attract flies, which is not so different from the smell of the unwashed genitals of a guy who wanked into his underwear three days ago. An unforgettable smell. *Phallus indusiatus*, commonly called the bamboo mushroom, bamboo pith, long net stinkhorn, crinoline stinkhorn or veiled lady, has an even more perverse look – it looks like a dick covered by a lace serviette, as it has a netlike coating around the fruiting body.

As an anecdote, I must mention that Carl Linnaeus, who gave the stinkhorn its Latin name, grouped it in the same genus with the morelle, calling it *Phallus esculentus,* an edible phallus. The name was later changed to *Morchella.*

The common stinkhorn has an extra-large phallus, as it usually reaches 25 cm (10 inches), the size of an XL dildo or a penis in some porn movies. Unfortunately, it has failed me as dildo, as it is very crumbly. Then I thought "at least it can be an ideal penis case, like the gourds covering penises in Papua New Guinea, as it is empty inside". Unfortunately, the cavity inside it is not large enough. Failure again… By the way, the Papuan penis gourds are usually made from a dried-out gourd (*Lagenaria siceraria*) although other species, such as *Nepenthes mirabilis*, are also used.

Potentially better dildos can be found in the plant world, having harder tissues than fungi. A cursory look at the world of pornography allows us a conclusion that the banana, cucumber and courgette (zucchini) are the three most common dildos. Scientific reports from hospitals add a few more species, e.g. Granny Smith apples so stuck in the anus that medical assistance was needed.

But these are all cultivated products. What about forests and meadows? It's not so easy to find a dildo in such places. Being a man, you would think that some broken wooden branches can work if well lubricated. But the ladies' answer is: "Never, do you want to hurt me?" It may be easier in tropical regions, where plants are so robust that petioles of large leaves or some inflorescences are often the ideal size. Their texture is softer than wood but harder than crumbly plants from colder climates. I know of an ethnographer who works in the jungle and sometimes uses the inflorescences of a *Philodendron giganteum* vine as a dildo (a plant from the Araceae family, shown below). These plants, together with other aroids, have penis-like inflorescences. This is reflected in the name of a related Araceae plant common in western and southern Europe, called lords-and-ladies (*Arum* spp.).

# Bugs

She was very excited and asked me to put my penis into her. When I did it, her face suddenly froze with terror.

"What if you infect me with something?"

"Like what?" I asked.

"You know, with your kind of lifestyle…"

"HIV? Chlamydia?" I asked.

"No, you know, you spend so much time in the woods, maybe you have Lyme disease from all those ticks."

She was partly right. I spend a lot of time in the woods and often get bitten by ticks. I have probably had ten thousand ticks on my body. There were once 20 stuck to my penis in just one day. The *Borrelia burgdorferi* bacteria responsible for Lyme disease can be transmitted sexually, but the chances are very low.

City people are paranoid about ticks, the demonic carriers of various, little known germs. The most familiar is *Borrelia,* which is actually one of the longest bacteria known, nearly large enough to be visible to the naked eye! The problem with Lyme disease is that the bacteria has slimy coating which makes it difficult to fight off for our immune system. It can also survive in its dormant state in the hidden corners of our body. I've been bitten by so many ticks that I am sure I have it. But I'm still alive and have not yet needed antibiotics for it. I think my body has reached a state of equilibrium with it. However, I would try an antibiotic therapy if some serious health issues occurred.

Once I ran a field cultural anthropology course for an international group of psychology students. We were eating delicious cauliflower soup when a Swedish girl took her T-shirt of in front of the class and asked me to take a tick out from under her breast. I had previously helped people with ticks on many other occasions. One day I heard a terrible scream in the bathroom of the house where I run my wild edible plants workshops:

"What's going on?" I asked.

"Lukasz, come in and help," a workshop participant said.

Inside the bathroom I saw the guy sitting on the toilet with his penis exposed and two female participants kneeling and trying to pluck out the tick from the shaft of his penis. Every time they approached him with pincers, he would scream like a wild animal. Eventually I had to do the job with my fingernails.

How to avoid ticks? First of all, avoid tall grass and areas overgrown by ferns. This is their main habitat. They are much less common in short meadows or clear forests deprived of undergrowth. In spite of this rule, I must say that I've caught quite a few ticks from lying in any grassland for a long time. So, after long and enjoyable sex, always do a general body check-up.

Ticks can allegedly be deterred by the smell of some plants, such as tansy (*Tanacetum vulgare*) and related species like pyrethrum daisy (*Tanacetum cinerariifolium*). Some people say citronella oil, lemon grass, or tea tree oil will work too. But what hungry tick could resist a yummy hot body, even if it smells of tansy?

The forest is full of dangers for our pleasure, which deters many people. Some creatures just lurk around, waiting for our body fluids and secretions containing valuable proteins. In Poland on a hot humid afternoon you will be attacked by mosquitoes and deer flies as soon as you take your shirt off. When you expose your genitals, even ordinary flies will join with curiosity. That is why I much prefer first warm early spring days when there are no leaves on the trees, when sap rushes through the stems of birches and maples, and you can expose yourself to the universe without the danger of being bitten. All these bugs have not hatched yet. I prefer getting a bit chilly in April than bitten in July.

Deer flies from the Tabanidae family are especially annoying. Here in Poland, we usually have *Chrysops caecutiens* and *Chrysops relictus.* Their females suck blood from mammals and attack people as well. Their larvae live in puddles and ponds. If you're near water on a hot day before a storm, the deer flies won't let you stay still for long. I associate summer sex in the Carpathians with my bum being bit and dripping with blood from their bites and from being scratched by brambles. On top of this, I am allergic to grasses… Every time my calves touch the flowers of grasses, a cloud of little red spots appears on them. In spite of this, I enjoy sex in nature and treat those stings and scratches as "natural" acupuncture. God knows how many energy channels they activate. For free. However, the presence of stinging insects does have an effect on the duration of sex, and it will definitely be more enjoyable for couples who come quicker. For those women who need a lot of time to achieve orgasm, the presence of their flying enemies probably won't help. Sometimes it is better to give up and say, "let's finish off at home or in the car."

Be positive. Not all insects which land on you bite. For example, many species of ordinary flies will just want to drink your salty sweat or genital juices. They will be particularly attracted by the semen. Normally only a dozen flies land on your penis once you orgasm. You have created a feast for them. Of course, I am talking from the perspective of someone who lives in a pocket of unspoiled countryside in

Eastern Europe. If you make love by a hedge of pesticide-ridden and wind-swept England, the flies may not turn up at all. Which is actually a shame.

When talking about flies and sex, one must not forget the Spanish fly (*Lytta vesicatoria*). It is actually not a fly at all but an emerald-green beetle from the blister beetle family (Meloidae). This animal is the source of the terpenoid cantharidin, a toxic blistering agent which was once used as an aphrodisiac and causes the swelling of genitals, including prolonged erection in men (priapism), and at the same time makes them more sensitive to pleasure. Occasionally other species from the Meloidae family were used for the same purpose. It is consumed orally. However, cantharidin is a deadly toxin and the use of the Spanish fly is banned in many countries. Spanish flies were sometimes a minor ingredient in the Northern African spice blend known as *ras el hanout*. The sale of these insects in Moroccan spice markets was made illegal in the 1990s.

A paste which contained hashish, almond paste, pistachio nuts, sugar, orange or tamarind peel, cloves, various other spices and occasionally the ground beetle, used to be made in North Africa. In the past, the Spanish fly was also added to food in Europe, for example in ancient Rome it was sometimes used secretly, without the knowledge of other people eating the meal. For example, as reported by the ancient Roman historian Tacitus, it was eaten by the empress Livia, the wife of Caesar Augustus. The French writer Marquis de Sade (1740–1814) is said to have accidentally poisoned prostitutes during an orgy by giving them aniseed-flavoured pastilles with Spanish flies.

Let's go back to the woods. Another kind of deer fly, also called deer ked (*Lipoptena cervi*), is a particular nuisance in my forest. This species from the Hippoboscidae family madly attacks eyeballs. It just flies on you and wants to get into your eyes, hair, skin. It can be found in the temperate zone of Eurasia. It is a parasite on roe deer, red deer and elk, living off their blood.

After finding the host, fertilized females give life to a larva which lives in the fur of animals. There are no reports of deer fly larvae living on humans, but their bites are quite dangerous. At first, they are hard to sense but later often develop into serious allergic reactions, which look a bit like the rosy circles on skin from tick bites.

Making love in the Scottish Highlands or the Siberian taiga can be even less fun. As soon as it gets a bit warmer in spring, swarms of midges (black flies, *Simulidae*) appear everywhere. These are various species of very small insects. Sometimes there are so many of these flies that they can cover your body and can even cause cattle to die. Special meshes are used to protect from them, but they have to be really fine to be efficient. People in Scotland used bog myrtle (*Myrica gale*) or grew lemon geranium (*Pelargnium* sp.) as scented deterrents.

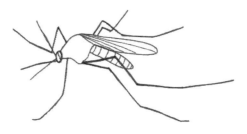

And then there are mosquitoes! They are particularly abundant and treacherous in humid tropical territories. They can also be a nuisance in my Polish motherland, where they are large enough to be easily spotted. They are much smaller in the tropics. Exposing your body parts feels nice in the gentle warmth of the evening, but just a few minutes later your whole body starts itching.

There can be something pleasant in the pain resulting from mosquito bites. If patient enough, you can actually make watching a mosquito bite your leg and suck your blood a meditative practice, which cannot be said of the attacks of deer flies or black flies.

And leeches… They are not so abundant in temperate climates, and their habitat is restricted to streams and ponds, but in the tropical climate they can even inhabit treetops. They fall from above and suck your blood without you even noticing. I remember a trek through southern Thailand where after five miles from the tropical forest, around Khaosok, my feet were covered with blood. Well, if you like the smell and taste of human blood, there's a feast for you.

A friend told me that, in order to make love in the forests of Indonesia, they once made circle of salt and lit lots of incense sticks inside it to keep most insects and leeches away. I have not tried this myself, though.

Love in the jungle is beautiful in a hammock. This book is about sex in nature, and hammocks make the experience less natural. So, I should stop, but hammocks are priceless in the wet tropics. By making love in a hammock, you will avoid at least 99% of scolopendras, snakes, scorpions, and spiders. I wonder how many children of the equatorial regions were conceived in one.

For those without a hammock, banana leaves or the leaves of several similar genera are a good option. They will provide a smooth and relatively safe base for you to lie on. Unfortunately, it feels more like a plastic tarpaulin than a woollen blanket.

Writing about the biting creatures I forgot ants. Ants have a lot in common with nettles, as in both cases it is a formic acid injection which causes the itching and blistering. In Poland, everyone's heard of sexual pleasures accompanied by ants through the 19th century verse novel by Adam Mickiewicz, called *Pan Tadeusz* (the full title being *Pan Tadeusz: or, The last foray in Lithuania, a story of life among Polish gentlefolk in the years 1811 and 1812, in twelve books*). This is a classic of Polish romanticism and contains a description of the rendezvous between a young and inexperienced lad, the main hero of the novel, and a slightly older and more experienced woman, Telimena, whose legs get covered by crawling ants. The helpful Tadeusz offers to remove them. The novel stays at this stage, but an unofficial continuation of the plot written by another 19th century writer, Antoni Ostrowski (1869-1921) entitled *Spotkanie się pana Tadeusza z Telimeną w Świątyni Dumania i zgoda ułatwiona za pośrednictwem mrówek* ("The meeting of Mr Tadeusz and Telimena at the Temple of Thoughts and their agreement facilitated by ants"), contains a very explicit description of what happens between the two while removing the ants in the garden.

Yes, ants can surprise you. They will surprise you when you least expect it, when you feel the biggest pleasure or just about when you were going to have your orgasm for which your partner worked for an hour.

They will usually sting you in the bum or hips. In Poland the red ant *Myrmica rufa* is usually the culprit.

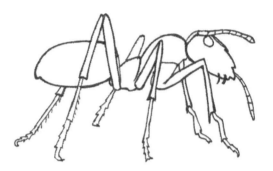

## Hitching a ride on the pussy

Have you heard of zoochory? No, it has nothing to do with zoophilia… This complicated scientific term means spreading plant seeds or fruits via animals. This method of dispersal can be divided into synzoochory, endozoochory and epizoochory. Synzoochory occurs when an animal carries a seed and deposits it or drops it somewhere, as jays and crows and squirrels do with nuts. Sometimes they forget about the seeds and fruits they've buried, no longer need them or just drop them. Endozoochory happens when a fruit (usually a fleshy fruit) is eaten and the seed is later excreted. As a rule, whole intact seeds survive the journey through the digestive tracts and germinate in the faeces/dung. We imagine they are beautiful berries swallowed by birds. But seeds germinate even in the dung of the bison, which consumes grasses and forest forbs. You also take part in endozoochory when you eat a mug full of strawberries while making love in the forest and then defecate like a wild person somewhere in the bushes. As for epizoochory: imagine a burdock fruit got stuck to your coat and you threw it out in your garden after going back from a walk. My friend, Mariusz Tchorek, once wrote me a whole letter about some burdock which travelled on his trousers from Norfolk, England to Dobre near Lublin, Poland. The supervisor of my master's thesis, Professor Janusz Faliński, once published an article reporting on numerous seeds stuck to his trousers. (Faliński, J.B., 1972. Anthropochory in xerothermic grasslands in the light of experimental data. Acta Societatis Botanicorum Poloniae, 41(3), pp. 357-368). Maybe one day a bur will attach itself to your body hair while you're returning from a morning swim in the lake and somehow will be left or thrown out a few miles further later in the day? Plants use mammals' fur and hair for long distance travel. Other plants which easily travel on hair are cleavers, also known as sticky willie (*Galium aparine*), agrimony (*Agrimonia*), Spanish needles (*Bidens*), enchanter's nightshade (*Circaea*) and devil's bit scabious (*Succisa pratensis*). Once during swimming in a pond, a spiny nut of water caltrop (*Trapa natas*) got attached to my pubic hair. It was an inch long (and bloody spiny), so I was well aware that I was carrying it. But if I were a deer or a duck, I may have decided to visit another pond and carry it with me. So, by not removing your body hair, you give plants a chance!

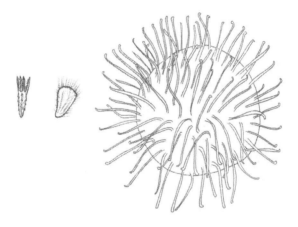

Plants which easily travel on hair (from left to right): devil's bit scabiuos (*Succisa*), agrimony (*Agrimonia*), burdock (*Arctium*)

## Natural lubricants

In many cultures, increased vaginal lubrication symbolizes a woman who has a lot of life energy. Only in some African countries do men want "dry sex" without these juices or lubrication, which is painful for women and makes it easier to spread HIV.

But how can you ease the friction without buying mass produced lubricant in a petrol station? Well, nature can help you…

You can try the caps of some slimy mushrooms (providing they are not poisonous…). *Suillus* is best. It is a common mushroom related to porcini (ceps) and it grows under conifers. In Slavic countries, they are called "butter mushrooms" (e.g. *maślaki* in Polish), as their caps are slimy. In some countries they were even used as grease for cart wheels… So why not use it as a lubricant? Well, don't leave all this slime under your foreskin after masturbation, as the next day your partner might scream, seeing the remnants of mushroom caps on your penis!

Another surprising lubricant is yew, or, to be more precise, its pinkish-red pseudo-fruits. In spite of the fact that its needles and wood are poisonous, the flesh of berry-looking pseudo-fruits is benign. Their texture is slimy and sticky, very much like penile secretion before ejaculation. I haven't read about this in any books. I just experiment with nature.

# In the frost

*In the meantime, the writer Lubisnki came back to reality from his ideal spheres and said in a dreamy way:*

*- (…) Would a woman like Luiza succumb her passion in a cheap hotel or an old sofa? A woman with such a rich soul needs something unusual, amazing, non-banal. And when I walked with you through the forest, and when I saw that Mr Porwasz knocked snow-covered branches with a thin stick and they straightened suddenly like soldiers in a parade, I thought then that Luiza could one day go for a walk with this woodcutter. He would break a thin stick and raise the branches in front of her, and she would notice in it something miraculous, magic, and she would suddenly want to free herself from the burden of her passions, and fulfil herself with the woodcutter somewhere in the forest, under branches heavy with snow.*

> — Zbigniew Nienacki, *Raz do roku w Skiroławkach [Once a year in Skiroławki]*, my translation from Polish

Sex in the snow is definitely something for the hot-bloodied. It's the best way to find out if a partner really turns you on or if a guy is really turned on by you, as it is quite difficult for a man to maintain an erection in the cold snow. The exposed penis quickly shrinks. So, it is best to insert it in a hot orifice straight away. Make love in a sheepskin coat. Quickly. Or prop yourself against a tree trunk and make love standing up.

## Into the mud

We walked through a lush meadow, partly to find mushrooms, partly to find a place for sex. She walked in front of me. The hot and humid summer day meant I could smell her from afar. We reached a small round pond in the middle of the meadow. We followed a trail made by animals. There were footprints of roe deer and wild boar.

We could not resist any more. We made love on the mud. I pressed her body into the wet clay, erasing the hoof-prints by pushing her back to and fro. The ground was so wet that she would disappear into the mud. At some point just the breasts, belly and knees stuck out of the mud. We became one with the Earth, ground, soil, mud, meadow and summer.

## Angkor Wat

Angor Wat is a ruined complex of temples in what is now Cambodia and one of the most amazing places I have ever seen. It was abandoned and overgrown by the jungle for hundreds of years. The overgrown, gigantic strangler fig trees and dipterocarps are like temples in themselves. The buildings impress you with the size and numbers, too. What is most amazing is how the trees and stone buildings merge, how the trees surround them and embrace them. Many of the trees have been cut to preserve the temples and make it possible to take photos of the architecture. The place has turned into some kind of landscape park. Of course, Angkor Wat looks better in photos than in reality due to the crowds of tourists it attracts.

I felt incredible sexual excitement caused by the presence of the encroaching tropical forest. I was missing someone, and I imagined us making love in the jungle, behind the trees. I moved 100 metres to the side and discovered that I entered a rain forest completely devoid of people. You could only hear some distant murmuring. I lay on the forest floor, my head propped against the trunk of a cotton tree (*Bombax ceiba*) with a gigantic wasp or bee nest hanging from one of its branches. I often see wild bees and wasp nests on this species, probably because the trunk has a lot of spines. These make it difficult to climb for people and animals. Then I realized tropical forests were not only my sexual fantasy, I could see there were a few condoms lying around.

What should you do with condoms in nature? It's best if you take them back to a city and dispose of them properly. Most male condoms are made of latex, which is a natural secretion from rubber trees. While latex is fully biodegradable, the decomposition may not be so easy, as they're also made with stabilizers, preservatives, and hardening agents. Plastic (polyurethane) condoms won't decompose. It's best to read the packet and check for recent developments. As the world is turning away from plastic, condoms will be more and more biodegradable. As a rule, don't leave it lying around on the surface. And remember about dogs or children who may encounter them.

The woman I was missing at the time had come to my workshops a few months before. Then she stayed over for a couple of days. It all started from drinking a Japanese dogwood (*Cornus kousa*) liqueur I made. It was in a jar filled by its raspberry-like pompon fruits. It was full moon on a chilly September night with temperatures going down to 5 °C. We got a two-person sleeping bag and walked in the moonlight into the centre of a large meadow.

# Sea

The pleasant scenery of a beach is probably one of the most common backgrounds of female nude stock photos. It is also commonly featured in internet porn when you type "sex in nature". We are all attracted to visiting sandy beaches, and the seashore as the edge of different elements, a place where water and land ecosystems meet, an ecotone. After all, it's children who drag their parents to stay by the beach, the parents who would sometimes rather go hiking or stay at home working in the garden.

Lying naked on a warm sandy beach with breeze gently blowing on you is ideal for a few minutes of nirvana. To stand it for an extended period of time, you're better off if you have suntan lotion and some experience in meditation. After 10 minutes, or an hour, or three hours at most, you will want to play with a ball, eat a burger or go for a walk. Sex can also be a nice break from complete inactivity, provided you are in an empty place. Apart from the openness and possibility of third parties being your unwanted witnesses, another problem with wallowing in the sand is its grains getting into your intimate places, scratching and making bruises and abrasions. You have to be careful, take a shower afterwards.

Sandy beaches are often accompanied by dunes. This is the case on the Polish or Lithuanian Baltic shore, in Normandy, parts of Scotland, and hundreds of other places. Dunes are often overgrown by tall grasses like *Leymus arenarius*. Sometimes these grasses are planted on purpose to stabilize the dunescape (civilization does not like changes of borders). These grassy dunes are an ideal hideaway for lovers. Much worse if the dunes are overgrown by spiny roses (*Rosa pimpinellifolia, R. rugosa*) or sea buckthorn (*Eleagnus rhamnoides*).

And what if the beach is stony? Then it is difficult to walk on it barefoot. And when you lie on it, squashed by your partner, it feels really uncomfortable. The trick is to find a large flat stone to lie on. Or to find a protruding stone and treat it like a chair. The sea shore is full of playful objects. You can sit on a stone, wrap seaweed around your body and pretend to be a mermaid, drinking the sperm of your lover from a large shell.

"Suntan" is a Greek film from 2016. It tells us about a middle-aged doctor who arrives to work on a Greek island. There he falls hopelessly in love with a 21-year-old hipster girl who is there for a month's holiday with her friend. The hedonists have sex wherever they want, on a beach, in the water or behind a stone wall. They fully explore the Greek island habitat.

At some point in the middle of the film, Ana seduces the poor doctor and has sex with him. The place looks ideal for making love: they are at a distance from the beach, but they can still see the sea. They are sheltered by a crooked Aleppo pine *(Pinus halapaensis)*. You can see that the ground underneath is barren, easy to lie on. Some aromatic bushes surround them from the sides. The feng-shui is perfect. The sun is shining. It is a shame that the guy ejaculates prematurely and his infatuation eventually leads to disaster.

## Nettles

Most lovers of sex in nature hate nettles. Even one tiny nettle can spoil your picnic. In Poland, we have only two species of nettles – common nettle (*Urtica dioica*) and dwarf nettle (*Urtica urens*) – but they both sting. The former is larger and grows nearly anywhere where soil is rich in nitrogen – in forests, parks and garden. The latter is now a bit rarer, a small annual which can be found mainly in gardens. It stings like hell, though. In the past, it often grew in gardens which had a lot of chickens or ducks. I remember it from childhood, growing in abundance together with fragrant pineapple weed (*Matricaria discoidea*).

Those who complain about nettles should be happy they are not in an American wood with poison ivy (*Toxicodendron radicans).* It's a vine which trails on the floor of North American forests and is a real nuisance there. People who touch it either get blisters and burns or a strong allergic reaction. It's easily completely overlooked and there are known cases of unfortunate lovers sitting on it in the forest floor. Another plant with a bad name is Caucasian hogweed, the two species *Heracelum sosonwsyi* and *Heracleum mantegazzianum*, which have been brought to Europe as large ornamental perennials and as fodder for animals. They have become very invasive in many parts of Europe, all the way from Scotland and Norway to Poland and Ukraine. Touching the sap often (but not always) causes severe blistering which has all the symptoms of a very severe sunburn. The mechanism is this: the plant excretes fouranocoumarins, substances which increase your skin's sensitivity to light. Thus, individuals with lighter skin are more vulnerable. It is especially dangerous on hot days – it may even emit furanocoumarins in the air! Fortunately, it's easy to notice thanks to its large leaves. Locals usually know about its location, but you must be very careful hiding in the thickets of Scottish rivers as the plant is very abundant there.

## Poetry

From all the world's greatest poets, it is probably Bolesław Leśmian (1877-1937) who comes closest to the energy and atmosphere of this book. His most prized volume of poems is called *Łąka,* a Polish word for meadow. The poem's smell of summer, flowers, grass; you can hear the insects. They often have erotic content and are about people meeting in the surroundings of nature. My favourite, and also the most famous one, is *W malinowym chruśniaku,* which can be roughly translated as *In raspberry thickets.* It is a description of lovers lying between raspberries "for hours". The lovers eat raspberries. "The new ones which arrived after the night". The female has fingers covered by raspberry juice which look like blood. Insects make music and cobwebs shine. The man is "wiping raspberries from the hand given to me/fruits full of the smell of your body".

Leśmian's poetry brings to mind an oneiric Russian film from 2012 by Aleksei Fedorchenko. It is set in the Mari El autonomous region in Russia, which is inhabited by Mari people. They are an autochthonous group in Russia, and probably the last pagan nation in Europe. The film features 23 different short erotic stories about Mari women. Some of them happen in nature, sex mixing with the environment: A man sleeps with a birch demon, a woman is punished for making love with her boyfriend under a holy birch, couples make love or talk about making love in gardens, fields and in the snow. One young woman witch, Onalcha, even has sex with the wind.

## Ecosexuality

Nature can excite in many ways. It is exciting to be with your lover in the heart of nature on your own, in peace and silence. But for some, it is also exciting to be in natural surroundings naked on your own and to masturbate in the tranquillity of unspoiled surroundings. Recently this association of nature and sex has been named ecosexuality. Sometimes we hear about people making love to trees and masturbating in treetops and lonely beaches.

Sometimes these people ostentatiously refuse to have offspring as a protest against what humanity has done to the Earth. They often do not even form couples. Many years ago, I met a crazy mystic in my region who drilled small holes in trees and put his semen there. The famous performer Marina Abramović once talked about an ancient Balkan ritual of fertilizing the Earth in spring with male semen. In 2005 she made an installation about it, called *Balkan Erotic Epic: Group of Men Copulating with the Earth.* Something similar used to occur in one of the islands of Oceania. In order to provide good growth for yams, they had to be sprinkled with male semen or men had to have sex with other men. Male and female relations in this particular part of the year were banned. Maybe now, when ejaculating in the forest, we can imagine that we give life to other forms of being by refraining from producing human offspring who will go on to destroy nature.

## Designing a love garden

My wild garden covers an entire hillside. I bought it long time ago, in 1997. For over 20 years, I have shaped it to preserve maximum biodiversity. Because I love to balance light and shade, it looks like an overgrown park. There are open meadows, old tree stands, solitary trees, clumps of shrubs, springs and ponds. I worked like any other creator of bucolic 18th and 19th century landscape gardens – I wanted to create an idyll, a paradise. Is this also a paradise for making love? Could we specially design "gardens of love"? "Forests of love?" Erotic gardens?

In the Renaissance and Baroque eras, an Italian garden would often have a *giardino segreto*, literally a "secret garden". This was a small, hidden section of a larger garden, originating from the Medieval walled *hortus conclusus*. Even the entrance was difficult to find. The garden was sheltered by buildings, tall walls or hedges, or trellises with climbers. Aromatic plants such as lavender, roses, or jasmine were often present there. They could be accompanied by some water features, sculptures and benches.

If we design larger spaces for lovers, we should make wildflower meadows, large open sunny spaces where they could make love on sun-scented grass. Such a grassland should be mown once a year to remove brambles and tall perennials. It should not be cut too often, not as often as English parks, as this would get rid of the flowers.

A forest made for lovers is full of ancient trees. They have large side branches on which the couples can sit or lie. It has a low undergrowth which does not hurt your feet. No brambles, cacti or nettles, but leaves, snowdrops or periwinkle. It is full of fallen logs from trees with smooth bark, a stream runs through it.

This kind of forest is different for ordinary plantations used for timber, where trees are too straight and too similar to each other. Here the trees are different and have a character, regardless of whether it is a boreal taiga or a tropical forest full of strangler figs. Here things should be big, crooked and playful.

The forest for lovers should have a large variety of fruits, which you can feed one another like in the garden of Eden. Actually, by having sex in nature we come closer to being in this place which we lost. I am shocked how many people have never had sex outdoors. They have an incredible inhibition and think it is sinful to do it outside the house. Maybe by having sex in nature we could return to a state before the Original Sin? It really depends on the interpretation of this biblical event. I hope you remember that it was when Eve and Adam ate the fruit from the Tree, they realized they were naked. This scene has been interpreted in so many ways that I will not dwell on it here. But I do think that by having sex under a tree and repeating this act we slowly go back and at some point, we forget our nakedness. I think it is easier to transform sex from sheer lust in a bedroom to an experience of loving all the creation if we do it close to a wet damp ground, close to a tree, surrounded by flowers, seeing the sky and bearing the flies which sit on us.

Shinrin-yoku (森林浴), which literally means forest bathing, originated in Japan in the early 1980s. It is seen as a form of nature therapy. By being in the forest we become calmer and more connected to the universe. I am sure we can extend this practice to our sexual life.

What I propose in this book is weaving forest bathing, ecosexuality and the notion of idyllic and paradise together. I think the psychological, spiritual and sensual practice of experiencing sex in different natural habitats is only in its beginning.

## Tree log trap

My female friend met a guy. They had already met up a few times. They talked about nature, arts, photography… and nothing. He didn't take her hand, didn't brush against her breasts, didn't offer to kiss her.

"Lukasz, help me, what shall I do?" pleaded the friend on the phone.

"Well," I said, "you need to find a forest with large fallen trees or at least one tree. Pack some sandwiches and of course condoms. You have to walk around the forest for forty minutes, not less, not more. And then find the log. Sit beside it saying you are tired and need to have a sandwich."

"Why is the log so important?" she asked.

"The log will give you a sense of security, you will have a cover from the back. You will sit close to each other. The presence of the log will suggest you both lean towards it."

"Will it work?"

"Yes, it will, just touch his arm".

"It worked!" she screamed on the phone a few days later! "It's like a cooking recipe"

"Yeah, it usually works, especially when you are an experienced cook, but sometimes something goes wrong. Still, it does usually work." I replied.

Printed in Great Britain
by Amazon